Rise Up!

Take Up Thy Bed and Walk!

Dr. Denice Jacklin Valentine

ISBN 979-8-89243-798-1 (paperback)
ISBN 979-8-89243-799-8 (digital)

Christian Faith Publishing
832 Park Avenue
Meadville, PA 16335
www.christianfaithpublishing.com

All Scriptures are taken from the King James Bible

Printed in the United States of America

Congratulations!

Because of your destiny, you have been led by the Holy Spirit to pick up this book. You are predestined to receive all the treasures written therein. Please don't stop reading until you have read the entire book. Please share it with your friends and loved ones.

Before you go any further, *let us pray*!

Dear Heavenly Father, thank You for blessing me with this book. Please help me to find all the treasures written therein. Lord, please give me the wisdom and understanding to apply these principles in my life. Make it plain, Lord, so that I can share these truths with others. Help me, Lord, to "rise up and walk" in these blessings so that I can be an asset to the kingdom of God.

In Jesus's name, amen!

Statement of Purpose

This book is divinely written to launch you into the highest level of living, which is "life lived in the kingdom of God where the King sits on the throne of your heart and rules."

This book is designed to erase all fear, doubt, and unbelief by increasing your faith in the *finished* work of Christ. When you finally perceive that God has already given you all things that pertain to life and godliness, your struggling days will be over. Instead of asking for the benefits, you will begin to boast in the Lord with praise, adoration, and thanksgiving, knowing that they are already yours. You will reign as kings and queens in this life as you walk in dominion over all the wiles of the enemy.

Upon receiving the truth that is written in this book, you are expected to "rise up and walk"! For the Bible demands that "when we come into the knowledge of the truth, walk therein"!

Tribute to
My Wonderful Husband,
Earnest L. Valentine Sr.

To my love, my joy, my friend, and companion, my pastor. You are the answer to my prayer. I asked the Lord for a saved husband, one who loves the Lord as much as I do. God blessed me with you. God gave me more than I asked for. I appreciate you. You have enriched my life with three more beautiful children, Cotina, Nyree, and Fella. A compliment you are to my life. To God be the glory for the life that I share with you!

Love,
Your wife, Jackie

TRIBUTE TO MY CHAMPIONS!

Oh! What blessings the Lord has bestowed upon me!
Lt. Colonel Marvin T. Blackstock, you were with me when I went through the worst times in my life. The time when I was going through my wilderness experience. You were there at a time when my mother and my father couldn't be there for me. During that time, you gave me a good reason to live, to pick up the pieces of my life and be the best mother I could be. When I felt all alone, I would talk to you while you were in my womb. Every time you would leap in my womb, it gave me joy. I would tell you what kind of man of God you were going to be. I told you that you would conquer every one of your enemies. Time won't permit me to tell you everything that's on my heart at this moment. But I want you to know that you have made me a very proud mother. What a fine young man you have turned out to be! *To God be the glory for all the things He has done for you!*

My second born: Chad Blackstock, the preacher! Oh, how you love the Word of God. You tapped into that same spiritual well that God has placed in my life. I see the Word that we've learned together, as you were growing up, exemplified in your life. What a blessing to have a son like you. Always thinking, growing, searching for meaning to everything that you have been taught. Always trying to excel in everything so that you can be the best that you can be. I bid you God's speed as you launch out into the deep and become that vessel that God can use in these last days to set the captives free! Just so you know, you have also made me a very proud mother! *To God be the glory for all the things He has done for you. Rise! Take up thy bed and walk!*

CONTENTS

FOREWORD

You Have the Power to Get Up

Life is a constant process of getting up. We lie down at night with the expectation of getting up. But sometimes, we are hit so hard that we feel powerless to get up. When we're going through storms in our lives, we sometimes feel all alone. We wonder if God even cares or even knows what we're going through. Sometimes, it seems like He's never going to answer our prayers. So we find ourselves begging God, and God is saying to us, "You take care of it! For behold, I give unto you power to tread on serpents and on scorpions and over all the power of the enemy, and nothing shall by any means hurt you." In other words, God is asking us, "What are you crying to me for? I have given you the power to get up!"

What the Body of Christ doesn't realize is that many times when we pray, we find ourselves asking God to do what He has already done. We sometimes think that just because the circumstances look contrary to our desired results, we think that our prayers have either not been answered or that it is a *no*. In our ignorance of the Finished Work of Christ, we just pray and wait for God to do something. Listen, people of God, our Father has given unto us all things that pertain to life and godliness (i.e., everything we need to live a happy and healthy life). He has equipped us with everything we need to successfully overcome the wiles of the enemy.

In John 5:6, it says that Jesus saw the impotent man in his condition and knew that he had been that way for a long time. This man, like most of us, was suffering from the lack of knowing that "he already had the power to get up." Because we are not aware of this fact, we are constantly asking God, "How long are you going to allow us to stay in this condition, or when are you going to deliver us?" And God is asking us the same question, "How long are you going to lie down under those lame conditions?" Our problem is, we are coming to Him expecting *Him* to get us up when He has already given us *the power to get up.*

The lame man was at the gate called Beautiful begging for alms. He asked Peter for money. Peter said, "Silver and gold have I none, but such as I have give I thee. *In the name of Jesus Christ of Nazareth, rise up and walk!*" In essence, he is saying, "I don't have money to give you, but I have something better than money." The "such as I have" is "the power to get up"! Peter knew that once the man got up and walked, he wouldn't have to beg any longer because the same power that got him up was the same power that would put money in his pocket.

Our focus has been on the wrong things. We have been begging God for things instead of asking God for His strength and power to rise above our circumstances. Sisters and brothers, I'm not praying for your healing, I'm not praying for lots of money, I'm not praying for numbers in your church, "but such as I have give I thee, in the name of Jesus Christ of Nazareth, rise up, take up thy bed, and walk!"

Sometimes you don't need prayer to wait for God to get you up; you just need to get up! Martha was expecting her brother Lazarus to get up on the Resurrection Day, but Jesus told her, "I am the Resurrection" now! In other words, you don't have to wait for the great getting up morning; I give you the power to get up right now. It is time for the church to rise above those things that are holding us down. Paul saw the need to know Him in the power of His resurrection.

Get up, people of God! The power has been invested in you! God said that He has given us His name, His word, and has shed His blood. That's enough! Now get up!

My dear sisters and brothers, the mere fact that you have picked up this book indicates to me that there are some areas in your life that you need to rise up from. Whatever you're struggling with, you will find the solution in this book! Let me just go ahead and tell you that the Word of the Lord says, "You have the power to get up!" I know that you may have struggled for a long time with your situation, but if you still have breath in your body, you can get up! You may be lame, and the doctor may have given you no hope, but God says, regardless of what anybody says, "You have the power to get up!" You may not have any legs, but God's Word never changes. You still have the power to get up! You may live in the ghetto and not have any money; you still have the power to get up! You may feel trapped in a homosexual or lesbianism lifestyle, but God's Word says you still have the power to get up! You may be hooked on drugs and alcohol, but you still have the power to get up!

You may have been thrown in the fiery furnace; you may even be in the lion's den. You may have been like Joseph, thrown into the pit, but you still have the power to get up! You may have failed in your marriage, but you still have the power to get up! You may have been molested, but you still have the power to get up! You may have had an abortion, but you still have the power to get up! You may be a pedophile, but you still have the power to get up! You may have murdered someone, but you still have the power to get up! For Jesus says when you were yet in your sins, Christ died for the ungodly. That's us! God is not limited by how bad our situations are. His blood reaches all of it. Jesus went down to bring us up! But you have to choose to get up! Come to yourself, my friend, and realize that you don't belong down there. If God wanted us to stay down, He would have stayed down, but instead, He got up, and when He did, He got up with all power in His hand and then turned around and gave it to us. Psalm 145:14 says, "The Lord upholdeth all that fall and raiseth up all those that be bowed down." Though your sins were like crimson stain, Christ has washed them as white as snow. *Get up! Rise up, people of God! Take up thy bed and walk!*

Notice that Jesus didn't tell the man to go to the doctor. He didn't tell him to pray three times a day, nor did He tell him that his condition was hereditary. In fact, Jesus didn't even try to diagnose the situation. He simply asked the impotent man, "Wilt thou be made whole?" In other words, He asked him, "What do you want?" When Jesus saw that he was trying to get to the pool to get healed, Jesus gave him three commands: first, to rise; second, to take up thy bed; and third, to walk!

Rise! Take Up Thy Bed and Walk!

(He Who the Son Sets Free Is Not "Free
in Need" But Is "Free Indeed")

"*Beloved, I wish above all things that thou mayest prosper and be in health*, even as thy soul prospers. For I rejoiced greatly when the brethren came and testified of the truth that is in thee, even as thou walkest in the truth. *I have no greater joy than to hear that my children walk in the truth*" (3 John 2–4).

I truly believe that the most earnest desire of the Father's heart today is that His children prosper and be in divine health. It is evident, according to His Word, that prosperity and divine health are top priorities. It is very clear that He desired it *above all things*! There is nothing that gives Him more joy than to see His children walking in the truth of His Word. That truth is, when Jesus saved us, He provided health, wealth, and peace. If we are going to please our Father, we should receive His truth and walk in it *now*!

Over two thousand years ago, Christ delivered us from the power of darkness and translated us into the rich kingdom of God's dear Son. Tragically, over two thousand years later, some of us, to a high degree, are still chained by the power of darkness (i.e., still in bondage to poverty, sickness, and disease). According to the Word of God, Jesus gave us authority to tread over all these things. Jesus said in Luke 10:19, "Behold, I give unto you power to tread on serpents, scorpions, and over all the power of the enemy, and nothing shall by any means hurt you." Our problem is that we have not truly believed this truth nor have we fully awakened to the fact that "*he whom the Son set free is (not free in need) but is free indeed.*"

It is imperative that the Body of Christ demonstrates the truth that we preach. If we truly believe, the manifested evidence will follow. The world will not only hear the truth, they will see the truth demonstrated by us! If we truly believe, the Bible says that signs and wonders will follow us just as they followed Jesus. In the eyes of the world, action speaks louder than words. In other words, the world is not looking for lip service; they are looking for work to follow. They are looking for the Jesus who took five loaves of bread and two little fishes and fed five thousand people with twelve baskets of food left over. They are looking for the Jesus that healed the sick, raised the dead, cast out demons, walked on the water, and spoke to the storm and it obeyed Him! They are looking for the Jesus who loved us so much that He died for us. The world is looking for the same Jesus that is described in the Bible is full of grace and truth! The only way that the world is going to see Him personified is when the glory of His Word is revealed in us, which is His very likeness.

God expects us to be living Epistles. In other words, our lives ought to preach every promise in the Bible. The world should be able to "look on us" and see healing, look on us and see prosperity, look on us and see love and peace. The world ought to see us dominating the law of sin and death, demonstrating to the world how good God is, feeding the hungry, and bringing others into the Body of Christ.

God expects us to do these things, but we must not fail to take an inventory of our own Christian walk, to make sure that we are also walking in that truth; thereby, being the victor and not the victim. It is good to tell the world that God is a healer, but are *you* healed? *It is good to tell the world that God will supply all your needs, but are your needs met?* In other words, *is it working for you?*

It was the revelation of this truth that compelled me to write this book. When God opened my eyes to this truth, that God has already delivered me from the power of darkness altogether and that He has already blessed me with all things that pertain to life, the reality as a true born-again Christian became real to me. That's when I, like the prodigal son, came to myself and realized that I was living beneath my privileges. I also noticed that I was not alone. Many of the members of the Body of Christ are living without this reality as well.

My desire to share the revelation of walking in the truth of God's Word was also a motivating factor in the production of this book. If you read this book and embrace the truth therein (as yours) and not just words on a page, you will never be the same. You are destined to prosper!

We are living in perilous times. We are living in times when the church, as well as the world, are plagued with incurable diseases, violence, sexual immorality, suicide, terrorists, wars, famines, etc. Though spiritual darkness is running rampant in this hour, the Body of Christ will be able to see her way through because of Jesus. Moses and Joshua were a light to the children of Israel, thereby, leading them through their perilous times. Just as Moses and Joshua were a great beacon of light to millions of Israelites, the Word of God, Jesus was and still is that great beacon of light to all men to lead us through our perilous times. Since Jesus is that true light that shines in the midst of the darkest times of our life, our Heavenly Father expects the Body of Christ to be that same light so that those who walk in darkness will be able to see their way through our example.

Even though times seem dark, this is still a great day for the children of God. God has made this day for us, and He expects us to rejoice and be glad in it. In order to rejoice and be glad, we must *awake* to our righteousness. *Awake* means to be aware! We have to be aware of the fact of what He has already given us and stand boldly before the world and our adversary and declare, "I will only believe the report of the Lord! I will not be exiled from the land that God has promised me! I am now going in to possess all that Jesus paid for me to have!"

Rise up, children of God, take up thy bed (which means to get out of your comfort zone), and start stepping into your blessing!

CHAPTER 1

Rise

To rise means to ascend above your present position. If we are going to rise above our present positions or conditions, it will have to first take place in our minds. The Bible tells us to "be not conformed to this world: but be ye transformed by the renewing of our minds, that we may prove what is that good and acceptable and perfect will of God." We cannot prove the good and acceptable and perfect will of God until we change our minds with the Word of God. Jesus (the Word) spoke to the impotent man's mind because that was where his first problem began. No doubt, because this man had been in that condition a long time, he had a sick mentality.

As I walk daily, it is very rare to meet people who will hold a decent conversation without talking about their illness or the death of their family members and friends. Their greetings are always followed by news of calamities. If you turn on the TV, what do you see? The world is geared toward filling our minds with the fear of death. This will keep our minds in a low place. That's why God said for us to set our affections on things above.

We have to rid ourselves of the sick mentality if we are going to walk in divine health. That's why God told us to guard our hearts with all diligence because out of it flows the issues of life. As quoted by Mary Eddy Baker, "Sickness is the image of a thought internalized and is imaged forth on our bodies." The Bible says, "As a man thinketh in his heart, so is he." That's why Jesus told us to renew our minds with the Word of God! God told us to put on the mind of Christ. He also told us to think about things that are honest and of good report. Jesus didn't think about sickness and disease because healing was always on His mind.

Another problem with the impotent man was that he was surrounded by people just like him. It is a known fact that your surroundings will affect your thinking. If we are going to rise up, then we need to hang around people with a purpose and a vision that will cause us to pull up from our present condition. People with purpose refuse to sit still. They are always striving to do better. *Move away from negativity. Move away from the chickens! You can't soar with the eagles pecking around with the chickens! Rid yourself of the chicken mentality!* A man cannot rise up until he begins to *think it up!* God said, "As a man thinketh in his heart, so is he." The power to achieve anything lies in a person's mind. The Bible says that God is able to do exceeding abundantly above all that we can ask or think according to the power that worketh in us. God is saying to His children, "If you can think it, I'll go further than that!"

God put the responsibility for our prosperity in our own hands. That's why we have to make some quality decisions about our lives. He has already provided for us, but it is up to us to receive it and walk in it. We have the power of choice. We have to decide whether we are going down or are we going to rise up! God gave us the power of choice when He told us that "Whatever we bind on earth, He will bind in heaven and whatsoever we loose on earth, He will loose in heaven." Instead of allowing the demon of lack, poverty, sin, sickness, and diseases to keep us down, we should choose to rise in rebellion against it, declaring, *"Sin has no more power over me!"*

CHAPTER 2

Take Up Thy Bed

The second command that Jesus gave the impotent man was, "Take up thy bed." Taking up your bed is equivalent to getting out of your comfort zone. A bed is designed to be a place for rest and relaxation. If you stay in bed too long, you'll become confined to it.

A bed is also designed to comfort you in whatever condition you're in. When we become too comfortable with our conditions, we don't see the need to fight for our right to change them. That's when we coerce ourselves into believing that "God will make a way." This is a true statement, but Satan's intentions are to cause us to overlook the fact that God has already made the way. If we think that it's all in the future, then we'll never receive it. We accepted that because we heard it most of our lives, and it sounded good. The devil is a lie! That's the lie that Satan always wants the Body of Christ to believe. He wants us to believe that it's all in the future. If we are always looking for God to do what He has already done, then we will never receive the blessings He has already given us. It's time to go ahead and receive, right now, what we have been looking for!

The Bible tells us that "God hath given unto us all things that pertain to life and godliness." We'll get these things through the knowledge of Him who has called us to glory and virtue. So since He has already given us all things that pertain to life and godliness, then why are we praying for what we already have? All we need to do is to look into His Word, find out what He has willed us, and just receive it by faith!

Thinking that our blessings are all in the future is not a good bed to rest in. The bed for us to rest in is knowing that God has already taken care of all that concerns us. If we realize that truth, it will relinquish all of our struggles. *So rise up and declare, "I'm not making my bed with the sick because I am healed. I'm not making my bed with the poor because I am rich. I'm not making my bed with the unrighteous because I am righteous!"*

A bed is also a place that all of us return to when our work is finished for the day. It is also a piece of furniture in which one may lie and sleep. When we are in bed asleep, we are not aware of anything that's going on around us. If we are not aware of our blessings, then we can't rise up and possess what we do have. God said that His children are destroyed for a lack of knowledge. Satan wants us to stay in the bed of ignorance because he is aware that the only way we can obtain these blessings is only through the knowledge of them.

Jesus commanded the impotent man to take up his bed so that he would not return to it. He had been too long in that bed of affliction. Once he made a decision to rise up in his mind and receive the will of God in his life, which is to be made whole, he got up and walked in the revelation that he received at Jesus's command! Our conditions may look impossible, but we are assured by the Word of God that nothing is impossible with God. We are not limited because of circumstances because through Christ, we can and we shall overcome them all.

So many of God's people have returned to the same prison that Christ has set them free from. After God used Moses to miraculously bring the children of Israel out of Egypt, they desired to go back because they ran into opposition. That's why God closed up the Red Sea that they came through on so that they wouldn't return.

People of God, some bridges need to be burned. God decided to take up that bed so that they could make it to the Promised Land. God will do the same for us. In order for us to reach our Promised Land, we must embrace the promises of God. One of our problems in the past is that we only allowed ourselves to reach a certain plateau and rest there. That's when we will find ourselves in a wilderness situation. Then we begin to grumble and complain about past issues and not pursue all that's ours. That's when we must put the past behind us and press! It takes more energy to press than to rest.

When God closed up the Red Sea, He consumed all of the children of Israel's enemies. He informed them that the enemies they saw then, they would not see anymore! Jesus declared the same thing to the Body of Christ when He went to hell and snatched the keys from Satan and rendered him powerless. He declared, "Behold, all power is given unto me both in heaven and on earth!" In other words, Jesus has all the power, and the devil doesn't have any. Jesus then turned around and gave us that same power to tread upon serpents, scorpions, and all the power of the enemy. So my question to the Body of Christ is, when are we going to awake to it? Jesus Christ has already defeated our enemy! The enemy that we have is called ignorance. Friends, I don't care what it looks like, the devil is still defeated! *So rise, take up your bed of fear, and walk by faith!*

Jesus approached the impotent man and merely said that since he wanted to be made whole, he just needed to "get up, take up thy bed, and walk in your desire," thereby, implying that it has already been done. Jesus didn't lay hands on him. He didn't give him any medicine. He just told him to get up because what he was experiencing was a lie from the pit of hell that had enlarged in his mind. Always remember, don't believe the lie! So all he needed to do was to rise, take up his bed of lies, and walk in the truth!

The problem that has held us back is our way of thinking. The Bible says, "as a man thinketh in his heart, so is he!" Notice the attitude that Jesus had when He came into the presence of the oppressed. He said on one occasion, "Go, show yourself to the priest," to Jairus's daughter, to the maid, "Arise," and to demons, "Come out of the man." To the five loaves and two fishes, He blessed, broke, and fed five thousand! Jesus knew that he was never limited by any circumstances. He called every circumstance what God said about it, no matter what it looked like. We need to take up the bed of stinking thinking and get a checkup from the neck up.

CHAPTER 3

Walk

The third command that Jesus gave the impotent man was to walk. Colossians 1:9–10: "For this cause we also, since the day we heard it, do not cease to pray for you, and to desire that ye might be filled with the knowledge of His will in all wisdom and spiritual understanding; that ye might walk worthy of the Lord unto all pleasing, being fruitful in every good work, and increasing in the knowledge of God."

Notice that in this verse of Scripture, Paul prayed first that we might be filled with the knowledge of God's will in wisdom and understanding so that we may have a pleasing lifestyle unto God. The Bible admonishes us, when we come into the knowledge of the truth, to walk therein. The prerequisite to walking in the truth is that we first know what the truth is. God expects us to walk worthy of Him! He hath delivered us from Satan's power. He went through hell to set us free, and He expects us to live in that freedom. Once the Body of Christ begins to walk in that freedom, she will exemplify that city whose builder and maker is God. We cannot do the work that Christ has left for us until we walk in that freedom. How can we glorify a free God while we are in bondage ourselves? We must walk in the authority of God's Word. When we begin to walk in the authority of His Word, we are ready for destiny.

When God builds a city, it stands firm. The fire shall not kindle upon it, and the flood shall not overtake it. It doesn't matter how impossible the situation may be. Jesus is still Lord. Don't hesitate, people of God, step out on God's Word! Rise, take up thy bed of affliction, and wave Jesus's bloodstained banner in the devil's face and say, "Jesus took my infirmities and carried my sorrows. He bore my sickness, and by every stripe that He carried on His back, I am healed!" So rejoice! Rise, take up thy bed, and walk!

CHAPTER 4

Why Sit We Here and Die

(When Faith Steps Up, God Steps In!)

Second Kings 7:3-4: "And there were four leprous men at the entering in of the gate; and they said one to another, Why sit we here and die? If we say, We will enter into the city, then the famine is in the city, and if we sit still here, we die also. Now therefore, come, and let us fall unto the host of the Syrians; if they save us alive, we shall live; and if they kill us, we shall but die."

If we're going to live, we have to move. If you sit still, you're going to die. I preached a message entitled "Don't Be a Sitting Duck." The lazy duck is always the perfect target. He will most likely be the first one to end up on somebody's dinner table. A moving target is more difficult to kill. God is looking for people who don't mind moving even if it's a life-threatening situation. Don't let fear paralyze your faith. Dare to believe the Word of God even if your life depends on it. When the Body of Christ steps out on faith the way those four lepers did, God will start moving on her behalf. When your faith matches the faith of Esther, "If I perish, I perish," the kingdom of God is yours! For the Bible says that the kingdom of heaven suffers violence, and the violent take it by force! And that force is the force of faith! If we want the kingdom of God, we have to take the force of faith, which is an action word, and get up and act on it. For the Bible admonishes us to be not faithless, but believing.

In order for the Body of Christ to walk in the blessings, we must get up and start moving toward our desires. We have an expected end, and we will reach it if we don't become complacent. God promised us that He would be with us all the way. Like the four lepers, sometimes we may not see how we are going to make it. Sometimes we will find ourselves between a rock and a hard place. When we find ourselves in this position, it should be looked upon as a God opportunity. It doesn't matter how hopeless a situation may seem, the solution lies in putting our faith into action, knowing that circumstances don't have any authority over the Word of God. When we get to the place where we will die trying, all of our impossibilities will become possibilities because *when faith steps up, God steps in!*

Sometimes circumstances may require us to walk on the wild side. If we keep on living, we will get a chance. Peter walked on the wild side when he walked on the water. He stepped out on the water with just a word from Jesus. Jesus didn't throw him a life jacket; He just told Him to come. Sometimes we have to walk the water to get to Him. Jesus is beckoning us to come. He won't let us sink. If we are going to rise to the next level, we will have to walk the water because if we keep doing what we've always done, we will keep getting what we've always got.

The four lepers took a walk on the wild side. They thought that since they were facing death either way, why not try to do something about their present condition? They felt that they had nothing to lose but everything to gain.

The four lepers had several strikes against them. First, they had leprosy; secondly, they were exiled from the public because of their sickness; thirdly, there was a famine in the land, which meant food was very scarce; and fourthly, the Syrian army, who was their enemy, was nearby. So the lepers decided to go into the enemy's camp not knowing whether the Syrian army would help them or kill them. They thought, *We might as well give it a try! They had the same spirit that Esther had, "If I perish, I perish!"* They said among themselves it was nonsense to just sit here and die without trying. Needless to say, when they started moving, God started moving. God ran the Syrian army away, and the lepers took the spoils. They had plenty of food and raiment for themselves and plenty to share with others. "You are not ready to live until you are ready to die!"

Sometimes we have to confront our enemy. It is necessary to let him know that we are not afraid of him. We need to fight the good fight of faith. That's why the Bible tells us to put on the whole armor of God so that we may be able to stand against the wiles of the devil.

The Body of Christ has to learn to trust in the Lord with all our heart and with all our soul if we are going to stand up in the face of adversity. God assures us that His Word will work for us. According to Isaiah 55:10, "For as the rain cometh down, and the snow from heaven, and returneth not thither, but watereth the earth, and maketh it bring forth and bud, that it may give seed to the sower, and bread to the eater. So shall my Word be that goeth forth out of my mouth: It shall not return unto me void, but it shall accomplish that which I please, and it shall prosper in the thing whereto I sent it." God said, "If I said it, *so shall it be!*" You can bank on it!

If you feel like your situation is overwhelming and you are too weak to fight, just remember, that you can do all things through Christ who strengthens you. So, let's rise up and run the devil off of our territory. Get up, man; get up, woman. Don't sit there and die; get up and make your demands and take charge. For Jesus has given us the power to deal with anything that the enemy is throwing at us. Don't be afraid, but Luke 10:19 says, "Behold, I give unto you power to tread on serpents and scorpions, and over all the power of the enemy: and nothing shall by any means hurt you." Don't sit there and be overtaken in circumstances when you have the power and authority to dominate it. *Why sit we here and die? You need to rise! Take up your bed of fear and walk!*

CHAPTER 5

Grow Up!

(When We Learn Better, We Do Better)

Galatians 4:1 says, "Now I say, that the heir, as long as he is a child, differeth nothing from a servant, though he be lord of all; but is under tutors and governors until the time appointed of the father. Even so we, when we were children, were in bondage under the elements of the world."

When children are born into a rich family, they are automatically rich even though they are not aware of it. The mission of the parents and teachers is to teach, train, lead, and guide them in the way that they are supposed to live. While under their supervision, children are expected to do as they are told to do, just like a servant. The Bible states, "When you come into the knowledge of the truth, walk therein." Whatever is taught to them, they are expected to live accordingly because what you are taught becomes the guiding force in your life.

At the moment of the new birth, God automatically became our Father, and we automatically became His heir. We became joint heirs with our brother Jesus Christ. According to our Father's will, we are entitled to everything that He has.

In nature, when a child is born, he or she has a keen sense of who their parents are, but their senses are very undeveloped. They come into this world helpless. They rely on their parents for everything.

From a natural standpoint, man was born into this earth realm first as a baby. In the eyesight of God, He created a man before the baby. God made man in His own image. God told man to be fruitful and multiply and have dominion and replenish this whole earth. Though man made some blunders along the way, God has not changed his job description.

Even though man may not have had the best teachers or earthly parents, he was still expected to carry out their orders. When God became his Father, He (God) expected him to walk in His orders too. Psalm 37:23 says that the steps of a righteous man are ordered by the Lord. God is expecting man to have the same mindset as Paul when he said that he counted all the things that he was taught before as dung so that he might receive the excellency of the knowledge of God, in Christ Jesus. Paul, in essence, was saying that he had to give His Heavenly Father's orders priority by putting away the old ways of doing things and doing it God's way.

It is normal to act like a child when you are a child, but it is abnormal for an adult to act that way. The apostle Paul said that when he was a child, he spoke as a child, he thought as a child; when he became a man, he put away childish things (1 Corinthians 13:11). The Body of Christ needs to grow up in all things.

We need to realize that God does not want us to remain servants. According to Galatians 4:1, being a servant is the same as being a child. When we were born into the family of God, we automatically became an heir of God and a joint heir with Jesus Christ. The new birth is just what it says, a newborn. That means you began as an immature, undeveloped child, not really knowing much. In the process of growing up, God will send you teachers and give you a manual, which is a Bible, to instruct you on how to live.

As mature sons and daughters of God, He expects great things from us. When we are children, He doesn't expect much. He doesn't expect an immature child to do a man's job. His parents don't expect him to run the family business, to drive a car, and certainly, he can't handle the bank account.

Until you've been trained and have reached the age of maturity, you will still remain in a servant's position because you have not proven yourself to be a mature adult. When you become a man, your job description changes. The Bible says, "To whom much is given, much is required."

As an immature child, we make blunders. When we make blunders, our teacher (the Holy Spirit) corrects us. When we receive our correction and learn from them, we make the first step toward maturity. Then when we reach a certain stage of growth, we will know what we are supposed to do. When we reach that level of maturity, we are expected to handle some things ourselves. No longer do we have to rely on our parents to feed us, to work for us, to buy our clothes, to drive us everywhere, to stop the bullies from picking on us, or to fight our battles for us. When we reach maturity, we do it ourselves.

In this Christian walk, the battle is not ours but the Lord's. The only battle that we face is having faith in what Jesus has already done. Until we begin to operate in this kind of faith, we are still powerless. The battle has already been fought and won for us. Jesus already wrought the victory for us and then gave the power or authority to us and then told us what to do. When we learn better, we are to do better. For the Bible says when you come into the knowledge of the truth, walk therein.

People of God, it is time to put away childish things and resume our position as kings and lords, like a child grows up and becomes an adult and takes authority over his own life and begins to reign. Let's rise, take up our bed of immaturity, and walk!

CHAPTER 6

Rise Up, Sons of God!

(Walk with the Air of an Heir)

Romans 8:14 states, "For as many as are led by the Spirit of God, they are the sons of God." This scripture clearly states that your father is whomever you obey. Jesus asked the question, "Why call ye me Lord, Lord, and do not what I say?" He also said to the Pharisees, "Ye are of your father, the devil, because they were obeying the devil."

As children of God, we must make sure that the Spirit of God is the guiding force in our lives. Are we being led by our flesh or by the Spirit of God? Are we Satan-driven people, or are we God-driven people? A child that listens to his father will get the blessings of his father. But the child that doesn't listen is disgraced. Romans 8:16 states that the Spirit itself bears witness with our spirit that we are the children of God, and if we are children, then heirs of God and joint heirs with Christ. If we are going to receive the blessings of our Father, we must be obedient.

For example, if you are the son of a rich man like Rockefeller, you will never walk in lack. Rockefeller may be a rich man, but his riches are no comparison to the riches of our Heavenly Father. In fact, our Heavenly Father owns Rockefeller and all that he has. So if Rockefeller knows how to take care of his son, how much more will our Heavenly Father take care of His own?

Jesus is God's heir. He walked with confidence, knowing that everything that His Father had belonged to Him. He knew that if He asked anything according to the will of His Father, His Father would do it. Jesus gave us the same privilege. He told us that if we ask anything in His name, our Heavenly Father would do it. The Bible calls us heirs and joint heirs with Jesus Christ. Knowing that we are His heirs, we need to *walk with the air of an heir*! The rich man's heirs never walk around like they don't have enough. They are confident that all of their needs are met. So they make plans knowing that everything they need to bring that plan to fruition is provided, and if it looks like they are going to fall short, they know that their father will always have their back.

Children are an extension and reflection of their parents. Our parents are usually our first teachers. They teach us what they know. The child resembles their parents not only in how they look but also imitates what they do. When we rise up and start acting like sons and daughters of God, we will be identified by the world as *sons and daughters of God* and not just ordinary people. The Bible says that the whole creation is waiting for the manifestation of the sons of God.

If you want to know what you are supposed to do, look at your brother Jesus. Jesus says, "I only do what I see my Father does." He is the prime example of what we should look like. He also demonstrated how we should act. It is very noticeable that Jesus never believed what He saw. He only believed what He said! Because He believed what He said, He saw it manifest before His own eyes. Jesus was not limited to lack, poverty, sickness, or disease. In fact, when He was faced with all these things, He called the sick healed, He called the poor rich, He said to the blind to see, He told the lame to walk, He told the dead to live, and to the demon-possessed, be free. The works that Jesus did weren't extraordinary because it was His method of operation. His method was the only thing that was real. To us, it was extraordinary because we had not witnessed such miracles.

In Genesis 1:26, God made man in His own image. He gave him dominion over all the earth. He also told man to subdue it. Man's job description was to have dominion, which means to have sovereign authority. To subdue means to conquer or bring into subjection. During Jesus' earthly ministry, He conquered every circumstance, even the devil himself. Jesus walked in complete authority over all circumstances and He expects the sons of God to do the same works. Jesus said, "I only do what I see my Father does." *So rise up, sons of God! Do like Jesus and take authority over sin, sickness, disease, lack, and poverty!*

It is imperative that the Body of Christ speak good things into their life because what we say can and will be used against us. Labels such as sick, lame, poor, broke, busted, disgusted, disease, murder, and iniquities were imposed on man by his own mouth. Obviously, God didn't create these labels because when He finished His creation, He took a good look at it and said, "It's all good." Now whose report are you going to believe?

It's now time for the sons of God to rise up and take their place. The kingdom is where we belong. Moving into the kingdom of God is a mindset of knowing who you are, whose you are, acting like it is so, and not allowing sin to reign over you in any capacity. The earnest expectation of the creature waited for the manifestation of the sons of God. The world is waiting for you! *So rise up, sons and daughters of God! Show the world who your daddy is!*

CHAPTER 7

Equipped

(Use It or Lose It)

Ephesians 6:11–18 tells us to "put on the whole armor of God, that ye may be able to stand against the wiles of the devil. For we wrestle not against flesh and blood, but against principalities, against powers, against the rulers of the darkness of this world, against spiritual wickedness in high places. Wherefore take unto you the whole armor of God that ye may be able to withstand in the evil day, and having on the breastplate of righteousness; and your feet shod with the preparation of the gospel of peace; above all, taking the shield of faith, wherewith ye shall be able to quench all the fiery darts of the wicked. And take the helmet of salvation, and the sword of the Spirit, which is the Word of God. Praying always with all prayer and supplication in the Spirit, and watching thereunto with all perseverance and supplication for all saints."

When a man or woman enters into the military, they don't go straight to war. The first order of business is to train and equip them for battle. The soldiers go through boot camp where they are rigorously trained mentally as well as physically on how to defeat the enemy. They are being prepared to win. The military makes doubly sure that they know who their enemy is and that they know that their enemy is nothing to play with. They teach them that their enemy is coming to steal, kill, and destroy. The soldier's mission is to get him before it gets them. Spiritually, we are engaged daily in spiritual warfare. Like the soldiers in the military, we have to be trained mentally and physically to win the war. The Bible tells us to be sober and vigilant because our adversary, the devil, goes about as a roaring lion, seeking whom he may devour.

A soldier never goes to war without his equipment. If he does, death is inevitable. You never leave home without it because it is like committing suicide. A soldier is required to put on every piece of his armor because every piece is necessary for his safety, and the safety of his country. The enemy is always looking for an open door. If you leave off just one piece of equipment, you become a perfect target. On the other hand, if you have prepared yourself and have put on your equipment, you can tell the devil to "bring it on"!

The first piece of equipment the Body of Christ needs to put on is *to have your loins girt about with truth!* According to *Webster's Dictionary*, *truth* is fidelity, accuracy, exactness, or conformity to fact or reality. Jesus says, "I am the way, the Truth, and the life." Our problem has been that we have been majoring in the facts instead of the truth. Facts are proven by natural circumstances. Truth is proven by the Word of God. We have to decide whether we are going to live by facts or live by the truth. It is not facts that are going to set us free; it is the truth. It may be a fact that I am sick, but the truth says that I am healed. I can't be sick and healed at the same time. The fact that I am sick does not negate the truth that I am healed. You see, people of God, the truth overrides the facts.

The second piece of armor is the *breastplate of righteousness*. This is needed to protect your chest. Behind your chest is your heart.

The Bible tells us to protect our hearts with all diligence because out of it flow the issues of life.

Righteousness means morally right or justifiable. God expects us to live on higher standards than the world we live in. We are to live according to the morals that we are taught out of God's Holy Word. God expects us to exemplify His standards in this world so that they can see Christ in us. We are also expected to be aware that we have a right to everything that the Bible says we have.

The third piece of armor is *our feet shod with the preparation of the gospel of peace*. God loves peacemakers. In fact, the whole plan of Salvation was implemented so that man would have peace with God. Since we have peace with God, then God expects us to have peace with one another. He expects the Body of Christ to reconcile the world with God, thereby, spreading the gospel of peace throughout the whole world.

The fourth piece of armor is to *take the shield of faith*. The Bible says that above all, to take the shield of faith to quench every fiery dart of the enemy. Without faith, it is impossible to please God. God told us in His Word that "the just shall live by faith." The only way we can overcome the enemy's devices is by faith.

The fifth piece of armor is *the helmet of salvation*. Our salvation is a crown to us. A helmet is used to protect your head because your head is where we get our direction from. The body can't do anything without first getting its direction from the head. In order for the body to operate properly, it must get its direction from the head.

The sixth piece of armor is *the sword of the Spirit*, which is the Word of God. In order to be a victorious Christian, you have to have the sword of the Spirit, which is the Word of God. Without the Word, we will live a defeated life. People would not be able to tell the difference between the saint and the sinner. The Bible says, "How can a man cleanse his way?" He answered it by the washing of the water by the Word of God.

The seventh piece of armor is *having a prayer life*! The Bible teaches us to pray without ceasing. A prayerless church is a powerless church. When we pray, the Lord hears us, and this gives him the right to work on our behalf, for the Bible says that the prayers of the righteous avail much.

The Bible tells us to watch as well as pray. We as believers are admonished to awake to our righteousness. In other words, come into the knowledge of it or be aware of it. The Bible also tells us to not be ignorant of the enemy's devices as well. He reminds us to be sober and vigilant because our adversary the devil goes about as a roaring lion seeking whom he may devour. This indicates that he can't devour everybody at his own will. He looks for someone who is not praying and has not awoken to their righteousness. Don't let that be you.

The eighth piece of armor is *to stand*! God wants us to stand up and represent. He doesn't want us to be like King Saul's army. When they saw Goliath, they were afraid and hid from him. God expects us to be like David and say, "Who is this uncircumcised Philistine? He doesn't have any covenant with God. How is it that he has the nerve to come against the armies of the Living God?" David knew that His God, who is always with him, was greater than Goliath. David was confident that God was his protection. He knew that God was on *his* side!

David remembered the time when the lion and the bear attacked one of his sheep, and God gave him the strength to overpower them. His faith was in the Almighty God, and he knew Him that way! He knew that greater was He that was on his side than he that was on Goliath's side. David said to Goliath, "You come to me with your sword and spear, but I come to you in the name of God!" David knew that if God be for him, then He is more than the world against him. So David laid Goliath down with one smooth stone of his faith, took Goliath's sword, cut off his head, and fed his carcass to the fowls of the air. We don't have to lay down in fear of our adversary. We must rise, stand up in the face of the adversary, and walk!

God is saying to the Body of Christ, "Don't come running to me with matters that you can handle yourself. Use the authority that I have given you, and put on the armor that I told you to put on! You can handle your own business."

Luke 10:19 says, "Behold, I give unto you power to tread on serpents and scorpions, and over all the power of the enemy; and nothing shall by any means hurt you!" *Use what you got!*

Sometimes our giants appear more ferocious than they really are. They want us to think that they're big and bad. If we do like David, we can reduce him with one smooth stone. All we need to do is take that little stone (faith) and hit the devil where it hurts and bring him down to his size. In other words, take that little faith and kill your own giant.

Children of God, we must realize that God wants us to go through to pave the way for others. Others went through so we could go through. So start stepping! God expects us to be trailblazers for the generations to come. So rise up and walk! We have the authority to use the Name that is above every name. We have the sword of the Spirit, which is the Word of God, and the precious blood of Jesus! *So start stepping! You have all the equipment that you need! Use it or lose it!*

CHAPTER 8

Going on to Perfection

(We Are Responsible for What the Next Generation Believes)

Hebrews 6:1–2 states, "Therefore, leaving the principles of the doctrine of Christ, let us go on unto perfection; not laying again the foundation of repentance from dead works and of faith toward God, of the doctrine of baptism and of laying on of hands, and of the resurrection from the dead, and eternal judgment."

Perfection is defined in *Webster's Dictionary* as the highest degree of excellence. This is the dimension that God expects us to reach. God said that He wants to take us from glory to glory and from faith to faith. The acts of the Old Testament prophets are glorious, and the acts of the New Testament apostles are even more glorious. Each generation exceeded the one before them. God is expecting our generation to be even more glorious because He has given us more. The Bible tells us that to whom much is given, much is required.

All of these things mentioned in this Scripture, such as the foundation of repentance from dead works, faith toward God, the doctrine of baptism, laying on of hands, resurrection from the dead, and eternal judgment, are the basic principles of the doctrine of Christ.

God doesn't want the Body of Christ to get caught up in the glory of these principles. These principles are to be appreciated because they are tools for the journey to help us reach our destination. He wants His people to follow them and pick up from where the prophets and apostles have left off. These foundations were laid for us to build on. God expects us to receive and respect them and move on. God wants the Body of Christ to know that these principles are only a foundation laid so that we can take it to the next level.

John the Baptist, Paul, Peter, and many more of his disciples were trailblazers for us to move into the next dimension that God expects us to live. These disciples, along with those names that were written in the Hall of Faith, taught the work with demonstration and power. They have clearly demonstrated that it works because we saw in the Word, the fruit that came about as a result of it. These principles should be the easiest to master because the vision was written and made so plain that even a child could understand and run with it. God doesn't expect us to be wandering with these things. God doesn't want us to waste time trying to lay them again. He wants us to take the torch and run with it so that we can torch the next generation.

We are responsible for what the next generation believes. In lieu of that, we must be good examples. Our foreparents taught us to hang on, and God will make a way, but God expects us to take it to the next level, preaching that God has made a way. We were also taught that when we get to heaven, we will shout our troubles over; when we get to heaven, we will be rich and in good health; when we get to heaven, everything will be howdy, howdy, but God told us that we don't have to wait till we get to heaven. We can have our needs met now, right here on this earth. Now is the day of our salvation! This is the day to rejoice. We don't have to wait until we get to heaven. We can have heaven right here on earth!

God Himself was the trailblazer for the first generation of Israelites. He went before them as a cloud by day and a fire by night. He personally revealed His love, power, and authority to them. He parted the Red Sea, fed them, and fought for them. God was their greatest advocate. He was grieved because, after all that He had shown them, they still didn't trust Him. When God told them to go in and possess the Promised Land, they refused because of fear, doubt, and unbelief. Instead of moving on the plan of God, they wandered in the wilderness for forty years. Because of their refusal, the first multitude, with the exception of Joshua and Caleb, died in the wilderness. Joshua led the next generation of Israelites into the Promised Land. They were successful in arriving because they had a mind to move when their leader told them to move. They were fearless and ready to face and conquer any challenge that got in their way.

We must get to know the vastness of God. We must see our God for Who He really is and know that He is limitless. He has no boundaries. There is no place where He is not. He can do anything but fail. If He decrees something, it is bound to come to pass.

God is a God on the move. It will do us well not to get caught up in our past failures or past victories. God is bigger than all that we have experienced. When God raised Jesus from the dead and saved us, it was the greatest thing that ever happened. We must always remember that God is Sovereign and is able to do exceeding, abundantly, above all that we can ask or think, according to the power that worketh in us!

The prophets and apostles were trailblazers in the wilderness crying, "Prepare ye the way of the Lord, make His path straight." Once these trailblazers laid the trail, they did not go back to lay the trail again, and they did not expect us to. They didn't see the need to go back and redo the grounds that others had laid for us. They just taught the work, received the work, walked in the work, and went to the next level of living. The Bible says in Hebrews 10:39, "But we are not of them who draw back unto perdition; but of them that believe to the saving of the soul."

The Body of Christ must stop wrestling with what has already been done. We need to take the advice from Jesus's mother, Mary; she said whatever He tells you to do, do it. We should just do it because Jesus says, "The works that I do shall ye (us) do also and greater works than these shall ye do because I go unto my Father." God expects greater works from every generation. He expects us to maximize every moment of our lives striving to fulfill our destiny, and our destiny is to rise and reveal God's glory. These greater works are the *rule of God in the lives of His people*, thereby, dominating the law of sin and death.

Philippians 3:13 states, "Brethren, I count not myself to have apprehended: but this one thing I do, forgetting those things which are behind, and reaching forth unto those things which are before, I press toward the mark for the prize of the high calling of God in Christ Jesus. Let us therefore, as many as be perfect, be thus minded: and if in anything ye be otherwise minded, God shall reveal even this unto you." So Zion is calling us to a higher place of praise. So rise! And walk into the next dimension of perfection.

Philippians 3:13 teaches us how to reach our destiny. The first thing he told us is that we shouldn't allow ourselves to get stuck in a rut by thinking that we have arrived because we have made great strides in our lives. We are admonished to forget those things that are behind us. In other words, don't let your past hinder your future. What was done in the past was sufficient for the past. This is a new day with new opportunities. After he told us to put past issues behind us, he told us to reach for those things that are before us. We need to seek God for all that He has for us and be ready and available to do all that He wants us to do. In order to reach, you have to stretch. If you have to reach for something, that means whatever you're reaching for is not at your fingertips. When you stretch, it sometimes becomes very uncomfortable and sometimes difficult. It is difficult because when you are stretching, you are trying to get something that's far from your reach. So that requires you to move out of your comfort zone.

When moving ahead, we sometimes feel the pull of everything that's behind us telling us, "You don't want to go there." That's the voice of the past. If you want to reach your destiny, you simply cannot listen to that voice.

The next order of business is to *press*! Pressing takes a lot of energy and force. It will make us sweat. The reason we have to press is because everything in our busy lives will get in our way. Discouragement will come from the north, south, east, and west. The first voice you will hear is, "You don't have money." The next voice you will hear is, "You don't have the time." The next voice you will hear is, "What if I fail?" That's when the demon of fear takes over. We have to press through all those voices to obtain the prize that Christ has for us. To overcome these voices, you will have to pick up the voice of God and decide whose voice you will listen to. When you find out what He says in His Word, pray for wisdom. Wisdom will lead you all the way and also eliminate all the frustration while you're on your journey. The enemies of our mind will always fill it with the reasons why you can't. Turn your "I can'ts" into "I cans," and rise! Go on because the Lord will perfect the work that He has already begun in your life!

CHAPTER 9

Grieve Not the Holy Spirit

(Unbelief Is Very Costly)

Hebrews 3:7–10: "Wherefore, as the Holy Ghost saith, Today, if ye will hear his voice, harden not your hearts, as in the provocation, in the day of temptation in the wilderness; When your fathers tempted me, proved me, and saw my works forty years. Wherefore I was grieved with that generation, and said, They do always err in their heart: and they have not known my ways. So I swore in my wrath, They shall not enter into my rest."

When God brought the children of Israel to the brink of the Promised Land, He told them to go in. They refused because of fear. It grieved God. The reason it grieved Him was that they experienced and saw His mighty acts. He fed them when they were hungry; He gave them water when they were thirsty; He parted the Red Sea for them. He protected them, and He fought for them. God became everything they needed. He was never too late but was always on time with their need. He demonstrated a God who was an ever-present help and promised them that He would never leave them nor forsake them. The Bible states that He gave them shoes that never wore out and kept sickness and disease from them. There was not a feeble one among those millions of Israelites. After all that God had done for them, they let fear, doubt, and unbelief keep them from the land that was promised to them. So God allowed them to wander in the wilderness for forty years. All of the first generation died in the wilderness, except for Joshua and Caleb. And they made it to the Promised Land because they dared to believe in God. We need to believe like Joshua and Caleb that if God be with us, then it doesn't matter who is against us. Since God is on our side, then we need to be on His side.

So many times, when we are challenged, we become bitter, disappointed, and afraid. We feel that bad things are not supposed to happen to us because we are Christians. It is the very opposite. The Bible tells us that many are the afflictions of the righteous, but the Lord delivers us out of them all. He also said, "In Me, ye shall have peace, but in the world, ye shall have tribulation." We have to realize that since we live in this world, these things will affect us, but we can face them with overcoming power if we listen to His (the Holy Spirit's) voice.

The Holy Spirit is our Comforter and our leader. His job description is to lead and guide us into all truth. He cannot lead us if we don't listen to Him. The Spirit of God is always saying to the church, "Let He that hath an ear, hear what the Spirit is saying to the churches." Sometimes we don't want to listen because we don't want our sins to be exposed, because we are aware that when our sins are exposed, we become responsible for doing something about them. When we are exposed to who God is and what He has already proven Himself to be, we are responsible for walking in the truth that we know.

According to *Webster's Dictionary*, to grieve means to cause to be sorrowful or to be distressed. Our mission is to glorify God by trusting and having faith in Him and doing the works that Jesus did. According to 3 John 4, the Spirit of God is saying, through Paul, "I have no greater joy than to hear that my children walk in the truth." Since walking in the truth is what gives Him joy, when we don't, it brings Him a lot of grief.

We have to come to the realization that "every temptation is an occasion to trust God." When evil shows up, we have to look at it as a God opportunity. It's a good opportunity for us to exercise our faith in God and for God to show forth His power and glory. Surely, sometimes these temptations seem like they will cause us to fall, but if we yield to the Word of God, there is no occasion for stumbling. We can stand even when all hell breaks loose.

There are so many areas in our lives that we need to improve in order to please God. The first thing we need to do is have faith in God. If we just believe God, all of the other negatives will fall off. God said that without faith, it is impossible to please Him. All God is asking the church to do is to just believe and trust Him because trusting and believing Him activates the Hand of God (i.e., it gives God the right or the go-ahead to work His Word on our behalf).

As children of God, we have to come to the realization that things are not what they look like. We may not look like we are rich, but we are; though we don't look like we are healed, we are; though we don't look like we are strong, we are; though we don't look like we have the victory, we have. It's not what it looks like, nor what the world says about us; *it's what God says.*

God saw the mess that the children of Israel got themselves into. Because of their unfaithfulness, God decided to kill all of the Israelites. Moses interceded for them by reminding God of His promises, and because of this, God turned His anger. Just as Moses interceded for the Israelites, Jesus intercedes for us, and Jesus expects us to do the same work for our brother.

On another occasion, God looked at the evil conditions of man and said that His Spirit would not always chide with man because he was evil continually. Because of man's evil conditions, God said that it grieved Him that He ever made man because what He saw in him was not in His original plan. He never meant for man to know evil anyway. God warned man of evil before he committed it. He told man, in the beginning, that it would cost him his life in union with Him.

God hates sin. Whatsoever is not of faith is sin. The only sin that will keep us from receiving from God is the sin of unbelief. It is a sin not to believe that God has saved you; it is a sin not to believe that God will take care of you; it is a sin not to believe that God has healed you. When I look at the conditions of mankind as well as the Body of Christ, I wonder if we believe and have faith in God like we say we do.

The Bible says that the Lord orders the steps of a righteous man. Sometimes we fail to walk in His orders and go our own way. It grieves Him. When we fall, we think that it's God's fault. The Bible says that God will not allow us to be tempted above that which we are able, but He will, with the temptation, make a way of escape so that we may be able to bear it. God provides a way of escape, but He does not force us to take it.

We have been taught over the years that all God requires is that we do our best. That sounds good, but our best is not what He asked for. The Bible states that it is required in a man that he is found faithful, walking in the orders that the Holy Spirit has set for us. When we don't walk in the instruction of God's Word, it grieves Him. If we want His blessings, we have to meet the requirements.

We are not to make decisions by our feelings but make them based on the Word of God. When we allow anything to override what His Word says about us, it grieves Him. When we don't believe what we preach, when we don't walk in prosperity, when we don't take authority over sin, when we don't walk in health, when we walk in fear, when we worry about everything, when we don't move when He says move, when we don't occupy until He comes, when we don't believe Him, *this is what grieves Him!* If anybody ought to believe and obey God, it should be the Body of Christ.

Unbelief is very costly. It will cost you your salvation. The Bible says that Jesus went to His own to bless them, but He couldn't do any mighty works because of their unbelief. You will never experience the benefits you are entitled to if you don't believe.

If Jesus had not invested His life for us to have all these blessings, it would not be quite as important to Him. He paid the ultimate price for us to have everything we needed. What more can man want or ever need from God? He told us that He hath given us all things that pertain to life and godliness through the knowledge of Him who hath called us to glory and virtue.

Because of the lack of knowledge of God's Word, God has been blamed for everything. He was blamed for the good and the bad.

When man charges God for the bad, it grieves Him because the Bible states that everything that He made was good, and bad was not included. When Satan succeeds in causing us to believe his lies, it paralyzes us in the battle against them. Satan knows that if we believe that God did it, we would certainly not fight against God.

Some of the lies that Satan told that somehow caused the Body of Christ to believe: God made me sick to show forth His glory. The poorer we are, the holier we are. Some believe that love is letting anything go on in the church. Some people believe that storms, hurricanes, earthquakes, etc. are acts of God. All of these are lies. Jesus said that He came that we might have life and have it more abundantly.

The Body of Christ has got to come to the conclusion that we're not going to believe the lie if we are going to please God. The Bible instructs us to cast down every imagination and every high thing that exalts itself against the knowledge of God and bring into captivity every thought to the obedience of Christ. Whatever we experience that is against the Word is not God. If it's not God, then cast it down and treat it like an armed robber.

God told us that we were going to have trials and tribulations, but the Lord promised us that He would deliver us out of them all. We don't have to be afraid of the darts of the enemy, for Christ, who is our big brother, has overcome the world. Because we have the greater one in us, we have the upper hand on the enemy. Greater is He that is within us than he that is in the world. Rise up, Body of Christ, and walk in the promises of God. Don't let trials, tribulations, and spiritual wickedness and powers keep you from receiving the promises of God.

I know that situations look hopeless sometimes, but they don't change the Word of God. God said, "Heaven and earth shall pass away but my Word will stand!" The Word, however, mixed with faith in it, will without a shadow of a doubt change the situation. The Spirit of God is groaning for us to rise up from the "I can't" mentality to the "I can" mentality. God wants us to boldly take authority on the earth. That's Christ's purpose for delivering us. He has given His body the authority to rule. We are in charge of the earth. He said, "Whatever *you* bind on earth, I will bind in heaven; whatever *you* loose on earth, I will loose in heaven." God has put whatever you choose to do in your hands. Grieve not the Holy Spirit. Receive the promises of God, move into the kingdom of God, and do something about what you believe. *So rise up, Body of Christ, and give Him joy! The Bible says that He has no greater joy than to hear that His children walk in the truth! Rise up, Body of Christ, take up thy bed of grief, and walk in the truth!*

CHAPTER 10

It's a Done Deal!

(If You Are Still Paying for Sin, Then the Devil Owes You a Refund)

Galatians 3:13 states, "Christ hath redeemed us from the curse of the law, being made a curse for us; for it is written, Cursed is everyone that hangeth on a tree: that the blessing of Abraham might come on the Gentiles through Jesus Christ; that we might receive the promise of the Spirit through faith."

When Jesus went to the cross, He hung there and cried out, "It is finished." He meant that He had completed His work. When He went to the cross, He completely destroyed the works of the devil. He paid for our sins, which indicates that we are debt-free! Being debt-free relinquishes us of all worry, thereby, providing the privilege for us to walk in full assurance of faith and victory over all the effects of sin.

If you are still paying the price of sin, then the devil owes you a refund. You need to cash in on it! If someone pays your debt for you, you become exempt from it. Since Christ has paid the debt owed for your sin, you don't owe the devil *nothing*. That's why Jesus instructs us to give no place to the devil, which implies that the only place that the devil has in your life is the place that you give him. Everything that exists because of sin has no power or authority over you.

You have a right to stand boldly and wave that blood-stained banner and boldly declare that because of the blood of Jesus, I am healed; because of His blood, I am delivered; because of His blood, I am set free. Because Jesus paid it all for us. If the effects of sin, such as disease, sickness, poverty, lack, etc., knock on your door; you don't have to receive the package because Christ has already redeemed us from them; therefore, *it's a done deal.*

On one side of the law are blessings, and if you keep them, you will be blessed. On the other side of the law are curses, and if you don't keep the law, then you will be cursed. The Body of Christ is not under the law but under grace. In the beginning, Adam broke the law, causing the curse to come upon us all. But Jesus became a curse for us so that He could break its power over us. According to Galatians 3:13, He became the curse so that the blessings of Abraham might come on us through Jesus Christ.

You might ask, what are the blessings of Abraham? Before I answer the question, you need to be aware that Abraham was a man of faith. To answer your question; the blessing of Abraham is the ability to believe God (i.e., to have strong faith in God). We have been blessed with the same ability to take God at His Word, regardless of any circumstance and just wait for the manifestation, knowing that everything that God has promised Abraham, He has also promised to us.

The spirit of faith is the ability to take the Word of God and use it to bless you in every area of your life. If you use it, you will see the manifestation of what you have faith in. And now that the same spirit of faith that Abraham had has come upon us, we have the power to speak and things will happen. We have the privilege to, according to Romans 10:9–10: "If thou shalt confess with thy mouth the Lord Jesus and believe in thine heart that God hath raised Him from the dead, thou shalt be saved."

Salvation is a manifestation of the spirit of faith. It's not just a ticket to heaven, but it is your title deed to divine health, divine wealth, and divine peace. So if you are saved, you're healed; if you are saved, you're rich; if you are saved, you have peace with God.

If you still believe that salvation is just a ticket to heaven and poverty and lack are a part of life, then that's what you will have because the Bible says that "all things are possible to him that believeth." Ask yourself, what do I really believe? Then look at what you have, because what you have is a manifestation of what you believe. So if you don't like what you have, then you need to change what you believe.

Salvation, as defined in *Webster's Dictionary*, is preservation from destruction or failure. As the Body of Christ, we need to literally believe that we are preserved from destruction or failure with all our heart in order to benefit from it. Before Jesus went to the cross, He healed the sick, cast out devils, walked on the water, gave sight to the blind, opened deaf ears, fed the hungry, raised the dead, spoke to the storms, and preached the Gospel to the poor. This is what the Lord has done for us. The reason we are still struggling with these demons is because of unbelief. We have not perfected our belief in what He has done for us.

All of these acts of kindness mentioned are what salvation is. It's equivalent to the devil starting a fire and Jesus putting it out. The Bible says that He hath given us all things that pertain to life and godliness, "through the knowledge of Him who hath called us to glory and virtue." He took care of everything that we needed so that we could live successful lives. When Jesus finished His work, He went to the cross and hung there and boldly declared, "It is finished." Since Jesus has finished His work, then why are we still crying out to God to do what He has already done? It's time for the Body of Christ to use the spirit of faith and consider the finished work of Jesus. Instead of begging God, we need to approach Him with thanksgiving for all the things He has done for us. We need to be asking God, "What shall I render unto You for all the benefits that You have given us?" For He hath done great things! Rise, Body of Christ, and realize *it's a done deal!*

CHAPTER 11

No Turning Back

(Don't Let Your Past Control Your Future)

Galatians 5:1: "Stand fast therefore in the liberty wherewith Christ hath made us free, and be not entangled again with the yoke of bondage." Jesus has set us free, but it is our choice to walk in it.

Hebrews 11:15: "And truly, if they had been mindful of that country from whence they came out, they might have had opportunity to have returned."

Philippians 4:19: "Forgetting those things which are behind, I press toward the mark for the prize of the high calling of God in Christ Jesus!"

To be mindful of a situation is to think about it continuously. If we get caught up in our past losses or our past victories, we will never reach our destiny. In fact, the grounds that we have covered that gave us the distance to look back, we will surely lose. In order to get ahead, we have to think ahead. The children of Israel kept longing for the bread of Egypt. If they could have returned, they would if God had not intervened.

We have to remind ourselves of the awesomeness of God. His legacy is more than enough to keep us in the game of life. It is good to meditate on His goodness. He is greater than awesome. There is always more with God. We can't put Him in a box. He is all-exceeding, abundant, and above. That's the God that's for us and in us.

The Bible tells us to lay aside every weight and every sin that doth so easily beset us and let us run this race with patience, looking unto Jesus, the author and finisher of our faith, who for the joy that was set before him endured the cross, despising the shame. In other words, He is telling us to get rid of anything that will hinder us from receiving all that Jesus has paid for us to have. He paid the ultimate price with his life. As we step out on faith into the things of God, Jesus will lead us every step of the way. Even when it looks like faith is not working for us, Jesus will help us finish our course.

Sometimes our past will hinder us if we allow it. It can be one of those heavy weights. The Bible admonishes us to lay our past aside. Don't let your past control your future. Instead, let it be a stepping stone toward your future. Let it work for your good. In Philippians 4:19, the Bible tells us to forget those things that are behind, let us reach toward those things that are before us, and press toward the mark for the prize of the high calling of God in Christ Jesus.

When you reach, God will reach! When you stretch, God will stretch! Just when the prodigal son came to himself and found out that all that was in his father's house was better, when he began to step toward his father, his father began to run toward him! That's what our Heavenly Father is looking for in sons and daughters who will truly lean and depend on and trust Him!

In order to enter our Father's kingdom, we have to denounce the slop of this world and sit at His table and eat as a son and not as a servant! Our Father is just waiting for all of His sons to put the slop of this world under our feet! *Move away from the troughs, get out of the pig pens, and move into the kingdom of God. We have to come to ourselves and declare, "I'm not eating slop any longer!"*

What is the slop of the world? Slop is rotten, odious food. If eaten, it could cause sickness, disease, and death. Food poisoning will cause death if the poison is not extricated from the body. Being conformed to the slop of this world is like eating food poisoning. If you are not transformed by the renewing of your mind, you will most likely continue to eat the slop. If you extricate it from your mind, you will only experience life. The slop of this world will only produce destruction. Sickness, diseases, poverty, lack, fornication, adultery, lies, backbiting, homosexuality, lesbianism, cheating, stealing, killing, drugs, alcohol, smoking, jealousy, envy, strife, and deception are slop. Don't eat of it!

Galatians 5:1 says, "Stand fast in the liberty that Christ has made us free." Stay free, Body of Christ. Don't let Satan bind you up again. Satan is still lying to the church. He is always selling us wolf tickets. He is a defeated foe. Christ has given us authority to put the devil under our feet where he belongs.

We have to be careful not to let our past control our future. Too often, the children of Israel looked back, longing for what they used to have. Lot's wife looked back, and it caused her to turn into a pillar of salt. It's not wise to look back while running your race. If you keep looking back, you will slow up your progress and never reach your destiny. It's okay to look back to see how far God has brought you, but it is not wise to want to go back. If you are always longing for your past blessings, you will never receive your future blessings.

Jesus has set us free, but it is our choice to walk in that freedom. Jesus opened up the prison doors for us when He took the keys from Satan. Jesus triumphed over the devil; thereby, rendering him powerless. Jesus declared that all power and authority is given unto Him both in heaven and on earth. Then Jesus turned around and gave the same keys to us, declaring, "Behold, which means to look or see; I give unto you power to tread on serpents and scorpions and upon all the power of the enemy, and nothing shall by any means hurt you."

We ought to boldly declare that we are not turning back! We are not of them who draw back. Drawing back is like a dog that returns to his own vomit. We are not going backward; we are pressing forward. *So rise up, Body of Christ, and make a platform on the devil's head, and walk on it.*

The sin debt has been paid in full. We don't owe Satan anything. If we don't awake to this fact, the effects of sin will continue to dominate our lives and cause us to go back to the same prison that Christ has set us free from. Keep your health, keep your wealth, and maintain your peace because that's what Jesus came to give back to us. Don't turn back because Christ has delivered us from it.

Jesus healed the sick, raised the dead, cast out devils, made the poor rich, gave us peace, opened blind eyes, and made the deaf to hear. *We are good to go.* Jesus has finished His work once and for all. He finished His work, and He is not going to make any more sacrifices for sin. As far as He is concerned, sin is powerless because He who had the power of sin and death is now rendered powerless.

The Bible tells us to persevere because our soul depends on it. Jesus says, if any man turns back, His soul has no pleasure in them. We need to get rid of the drawback spirit in order to persevere in the saving of the soul. If we don't know by now, what Christ has made us free from, look to the Word of God and receive it, and then rise, take up your bed of ignorance, and walk in your liberty. He whom the Son set free is free indeed. Rise! Take up your bed and walk!

CHAPTER 12

You Can Bank on It

(The Proof Is in the Pudding)

Malachi 3:10 says, "Bring ye all the tithes into the storehouse, that there may be meat in mine house, and prove me now herewith, saith the Lord of hosts, if I will not open you the windows of heaven, and pour you out a blessing, that there shall not be room enough to receive it."

The first command in this scripture is *bring*. It is important that we follow the Master's orders. What we do activates what God does. Jesus said, "Whatever you bind on earth I will bind in heaven, and whatever you loose on earth I will loose in heaven." If you don't do anything, then God is not going to do anything.

The proof of God's Word will manifest if you follow the instructions. The proof is in the pudding. In other words, you will never really know for yourself that it works until you prove Him. Put Him to the test. Take Him at His Word. His Word will bring a great harvest if you plant it. Please don't wonder about it. Just do it! Even if it seems off the wall. Like Mary said, "Whatever He says to you, do it!" God said that heaven and earth will pass away but My Word will stand forever. Just do it. "Try me and see!" saith the Lord. "If I won't open up the windows of heaven and pour you out a blessing, that there shall not be room enough to receive it." He also said, "So as the rain cometh down from heaven and watereth the earth that it may bring forth bud…so shall my Word be that goeth out of my mouth, it shall not return unto me void, but it shall accomplish that which I please, and it shall prosper in the thing whereto I sent it!"

God has deposited His Word for us. It's been there for over two thousand years. Just imagine the interest built up on His deposit. We need to take His checkbook (the Bible) to the bank of heaven and draw out. Everything that we need is deposited in the bank. The only reason you don't have what's in there is because either you don't know or you don't take the initiative to make a withdrawal.

When we begin to walk by faith, we need to keep in mind that things are not what they seem to be. Things may look impossible. It may look like you're failing, but God can take an impossible situation and make it possible. We must always remember that there is nothing too hard for God.

When we are expecting God to pour out His blessings on us, sometimes the evidence seems very small. But where there is a sprinkle, there is a possibility of a downpour. It's not what it looks like. All things are possible to him that believeth. We have to believe that nothing is impossible with God. So rise up, Body of Christ, and bank on His Word. *Take up your bed of poverty and lack, and walk under the open windows of abundance! Just do it!*

God's Word is a good investment for everything that we need in order to live a happy, healthy, successful life. His Word is healing, for the Bible says that His Word is life to those who find it and health to all their flesh. Wherever you plant the Word, it will bring a handsome increase. It is the best friend and companion that you could ever have. When you find yourself between a rock and a hard place, the Word will bring you into that secret place with God. He will hide you in His pavilion. The Word will bring you so much comfort. Even when you go through the storm, the Word of God will speak to the storm and say, "Peace, be still," and it will obey.

CHAPTER 13

I'm Not Going Down with the World

John 16:33 states, "These things I have spoken unto you, that in Me ye might have peace. In the world ye shall have tribulation: but be of good cheer; I have overcome the world." The Bible tells us that perilous times will come. Today, the Bible fulfills itself because perilous times are here now. The word *perilous*, according to *Webster's Dictionary*, means dangerous or hazardous. It also means exposure to injury or destruction. The Body of Christ is exposed to destruction as well as the world, but we don't have to go down with the world. The Lord made this day for the Children of God, and we can rejoice and be glad in this day.

We are living in an era when the effects of sin are running rampant on this earth, such as being plagued by incurable diseases, sexual immorality in the pulpits, babies killing babies, mothers killing their kids, mass murders, abortion, suicidal terrorists, earthquakes in different places, a lack of school teachers because of dangerous students, drive-by shootings, and a high disrespect for clergy (church). The battle between good and evil is on as never before. We are living in a time when men and women are calling evil good and good evil. Christianity is under attack more than any other religion. If we even speak the Name of Jesus Christ in certain places, we are subject to persecution in one way or another. We may even lose our jobs because of that name.

In America, we are living in the land of abundance. The misuse of abundance is killing us. We are living in a time when the church is mixing with the world. God gave us this abundance to establish His covenant on this earth. The world is taking the wealth in this nation and heaping it upon their own lust. Some churches are doing the same thing. If we don't take heed to God's Word and use the wealth wisely, we will lose it.

The Body of Christ must make a decree that we are not going down with the world, for the Bible says that we will reign as kings in life because He has overcome the world. In other words, we don't have to worry about all the calamity that has come and is to come because our Lord and Savior has already overcome its power and designated that same power and authority to us! Jesus has made it easy for us.

CHAPTER 14

Walking into Your Destiny

(Walking into Your Destiny Is to Do the Works of
Christ and Do Greater Works [John 14:12])

Ephesians 1:11–12: "To whom (Christ) also we have obtained
an inheritance, being predestinated according to the purpose of
Him who worketh all things after the counsel of His own will; that
we should be to the praise of His glory, who first trusted in Christ."

Destiny is a predetermined course of events often held to be a
resistless power. According to Ephesians 1:11–12, the Body of Christ
was predestined to be the praise of His (Christ's) glory. We may not
look like Him right now, but we are striving to be, and we are destined to conform to be just like Him. The praise of Christ's glory is
the very representation of Him on this earth. Jesus was our example;
He demonstrated our job description during His earthly ministry.

Christ walked in authority. He was confident in His Father in
all things. He dominated the law of sin and death. He walked in
love. He was a need meter. He changed circumstances. His presence
always made a difference. He led a sacrificial life. His life was dedi-
cated only to pleasing His Father. Like Jesus, we are to glorify God

in all things. The world should look on us and experience the presence of the Lord. Being all that Jesus was and doing all that He did, and greater works than He did is our destiny. Everywhere we go, we should be sought after because His glory is seen upon us.

Everywhere He went, He was a blessing. He opened blind eyes. He made the lame to walk. The sick were healed. Demons were cast out. He fed the hungry. He made the difference. Multitudes sought after Him because they knew that He could and would make a difference in their situation. When they came into His presence, something good was going to happen. If they had a problem, when they arrived, they were confident that they would leave with the solution.

When John the Baptist was in prison, he sent two of his disciples to Jesus to ask the question, "Art thou He that should come, or do we look for another?" Jesus responded, "Go and show John again those things which ye do hear and see: and what you see is the blind receive their sight, and the lame walk, the lepers are cleansed, and the deaf hear, the dead are raised up, and the poor have the Gospel preached to them." In other words, Jesus was saying, "If I'm present, then these things will happen because this is what I do and this is what I'm all about. This is what I'm destined to walk in." This is the praise of His glory.

Wherever the Spirit of the Lord is, there is liberty. God is about setting the captives free of all these enemies. If we don't see these things happening, then He is not present. For in His presence, there is fullness of joy, and at His right hand, there are pleasures forevermore.

Our destiny is to do the works of Christ and greater works! So rise up, Christians, and walk!

CHAPTER 15

Walking in Your Wealthy Place

Psalm 66:12: "Thou (God) hast caused men to ride over our heads; we went through the fire and through water: but thou bringest us out into a wealthy place."

Colossians 1:13: "Who (Christ) hath delivered us from the power of darkness, and hath translated us into the Kingdom of His dear Son."

Second Peter 1:2–4: "Grace and peace be multiplied unto you through the knowledge of God, and of Jesus our Lord, according as His divine power hath given unto us all things that pertain unto life and godliness, through the knowledge of Him that hath called us to glory and virtue, whereby are given unto us exceeding great and precious promises: that by these ye might be partakers of the divine nature, having escaped the corruption that is in the world through lust."

Deuteronomy 8:18: "But thou shalt remember the Lord thy God, for it is He that giveth thee power to get wealth, that He may establish His covenant which He swore unto thy fathers, as it is this day."

Psalm 34:10: "The young lions do lack and suffer hunger, but they that seek the Lord shall not want any good thing!"

These are just a few dynamic Scriptures that inform us of our healthiness and wealthiness. Please notice that in 2 Peter 1, our healthiness is predicated on our knowledge of God and of Jesus our Lord. We need to have a working knowledge of the fact that everything that He has promised us and embrace them as ours. Please notice in verse 2 that He has given us all things that pertain to life and godliness. Lastly, please notice in verse 3 that we have been called to glorify God in walking in our wealthy place.

You might have to go through the storm and the rain, but you can be victorious if you believe. God said in Isaiah 43:2, "When thou passest through the waters, they shall not overtake thee; and through the rivers, they shall not overflow thee; when thou walkest through the fire, thou shalt not be burned; neither shall the flame kindle upon thee." Sometimes God will allow us to be oppressed by the wicked. Sometimes we find ourselves enslaved by unfair laws. Sometimes on our jobs, we are discriminated against with our wages, and sometimes we are discriminated against because of our gender and our color. When God says it's enough, it's enough! Jacob was mistreated by his father-in-law. He cheated him on his wages ten times. Jacob knew that he was being cheated. He held his peace because he knew what the Lord had promised him, and that it was only a matter of time before God would bring him out of that situation. He knew that working for his father-in-law was only for a season because God had already told him of his destiny to walk in his wealthy place.

People of God, we are destined to walk in wealth and healthiness because of what God has promised us. In due season, God will see to it that we walk in that place. It doesn't matter what situations we are experiencing. In difficult situations, we must remain focused and prayerful. If our hearts are perfect toward God when we pray, God will hear our prayer and bring us out of bondage. Like the Children of Israel, God will not only bring us out to just survive; He will bring us to a wealthy place. He will deliver us from those slave masters and translate us into His kingdom. His kingdom is a wealthy place. His kingdom is a place where all the occupants live in assurance that their King supplies all of their needs, not according to the world's system, but according to His riches in glory by Christ Jesus.

Don't worry about what might happen; just consider what has already happened. Jesus died for our poverty so that we might be rich. *So start stepping! Rise up and walk!* In other words, Jesus took on my low places so that I might walk in my high places.

We are called to walk in our wealthy place. It's not all about money. It's about walking and living according to God's Word. It's about taking the Word of God and depending on it to work in all areas of our lives. Money is fleeting, but the Word of God will never leave us nor forsake us. If we learn how to put our faith and trust in the Word of God, money will come from the north, south, east, and west to supply our needs.

We are not wealthy because of our material possessions; we are wealthy because of what God says about us. Esau cried bitterly because his father had spoken the blessing that was due him to his brother Jacob. He pleaded with his father for at least one blessing. You see, it wasn't the material things that were important to Esau; it was what his father spoke into his life. If you want to walk into your wealthy place, find out what your Heavenly Father said about you. Receive it and walk in it.

We are destined to the throne of God. So we need to occupy our position as kings and rule, and that is really what kings are supposed to do. When you begin to occupy your position as king, your faith will be tried. If you stand, regardless of adversity, you will arrive at your wealthy place. Stand in the face of adversity and say, "I believe the report of the Lord. It's God's Word or nothing at all!"

CHAPTER 16

Be Kingdom-Minded

(In This Hour, It's Not Tell; It's Show and Tell!)

Romans 14:17 states, "For the kingdom of God is not meat and drink but righteousness, peace, and joy in the Holy Ghost."

To be kingdom-minded is to have the mindset that says, "I am everything that the King says I am, and I have rights to everything that's in the kingdom's domain."

A *kingdom*, according to *Webster's Dictionary*, is a realm in which God's will is fulfilled or a realm or region in which something or someone is dominant. A kingdom mind is a mindset to rule and dominate. This mindset says, "I call the shots." I'm in control. It is easy for us to believe that God is in control, but we need to realize that He is in control only as much as we give Him control in our lives.

For the Christian, the realm in which God rules is the realm of our mind and our heart. He sent the agent, the Holy Spirit, to live in us so that we will have that authority and the boldness that we need to rule and dominate the law of sin and death in this world. God wants to sit on the throne of our hearts to rule on this earth so that the world would know that there is only one King. He wants everybody to know that He is the King of kings and the Lord of lords! He is the one and only, the Alpha and Omega, the Beginning and the End.

The only way the world will see Him as King of kings and Lord of lords is when the Body of Christ exemplifies Him on this earth. We are His representation on this earth. We are in His stead; in other words, we are Christians on this earth, which means little Christ. We have to be whom we preach about. We should be like the disciples when they told those multitudes following them, saying, "Look on us." Before we can make this invitation, we must be something to look at, and it has to be different and better than what the unbeliever is used to seeing.

Realistically, the world will see Jesus when we become His representative on this earth! If we are going to tell the world how to do it, then we ought to show them how to do it. In this hour, it's not just "tell," but it's "show and tell."

We have to constantly make sure that after we have preached to others, we do not fall after the same example of unbelief. If we preach that God is good, then we ought to "be" the good that God is! If we preach prosperity, then we ought to be prosperous. Preaching with demonstration is more powerful than mere words because when the world sees that it works for us, they are more apt to follow our example.

The Bible says, "Let this mind be in you, which was also in Christ Jesus" (Philippians 2:6). Verse 4 says to look not on every man on his own things, but every man also on the things of others. When being in the form of God, thought it not robbery to be called equal with God. Jesus came to reveal God, our Heavenly Father, on this earth. He knew that in order for Him to reveal His Father, He had to do what His Father did. God is the Abba Father to His children! Jesus, knowing this, had to be Father on this earth. He told His disciples, "If you have seen me, then you have seen the Father." We are expected by God to have the same concept because Jesus told us that the works that He did, we shall do them also and even greater works. We have to "be" all that He is in order to represent Him on earth.

God wants His children to know Him in a personal way. He wanted them to know that He was sovereign and the Supreme Ruler over all. When God brought the children of Israel out of Egypt, He set up confrontations with Pharaoh so that He could reveal His glory to mankind. He gave Himself the opportunity to do miracles. He hardened Pharaoh's heart over and over so that He would have more opportunity to show forth His mighty acts.

Being kingdom-minded means to know with assurance that God rules over all circumstances. Because Jesus was kingdom-minded, He was never overcome with fear of any negative circumstance. He knew that He was in control and His Father always had His back. On one occasion, He prayed at Lazarus's tomb, saying to His Father, "I knew that thou hearest me always." He also knew that He really didn't have to rely on God to raise Lazarus because He had authority from God to do it Himself. He said, "But for the unbeliever's sake, He prayed to the Father so that the believer would believe and trust in His Father when they witnessed how God answered Jesus's prayer.

Jesus knew that He had the keys to the kingdom. Having these keys gave Him authority to move heaven and earth so that whatsoever He bound on earth, His Father would bind it in heaven and whatsoever He loosed on earth, His Father would loose it in heaven. He knew that since God was for Him, then no one could be against Him. The same keys that Jesus used to move heaven and earth have been given to us. There are no doors to the kingdom of God that we can't open. John 3:3 says, "Jesus replied, 'Very truly, I tell you, no one can see the Kingdom of God unless they are born again.'" The Body of Christ is not under the law but under grace, and no one can see or enter the kingdom except he be born again. The keys are only given to the children of God. If you want to get in, *rise up and walk, people of God. You have the whole host of heaven backing you up! Start stepping!*

CHAPTER 17

Escaping the Corruption That's in the World

(Let Not Sin Reign in Your Mortal Body)

Second Peter 1:3–4: "According as His divine power hath given unto us all things that pertain unto life and godliness, through the knowledge of Him that hath called us to glory and virtue: whereby are given unto us exceeding great and precious promises: that by these ye might be partakers of the divine nature, having escaped the corruption that is in the world through lust."

Jesus's ultimate desire is that His body be partaker of His divine nature so that it can escape the corruption that is in this world. His divine nature is all that He is. All that He is, is good. There is no corruption in good. The Bible informs us that Jesus made it possible for us to partake of His nature by giving us exceeding, great, and precious promises. Though Jesus went to great lengths to provide these great blessings for us, we have to choose to partake of them. The only way we can escape the corruption that is in the world is that we renew our minds with the Word of God. In other words, we need to get the corruption out of our minds. The battleground between good and evil is in our minds. If we only give place or thought to good, then good will cause us to escape evil. When evil thoughts come out of our hearts and minds, we are admonished to cast them down.

We do not have to live a corrupt life. According to the Bible, everything that we need in order to live a good life, Christ has already given us. It was promised to us in His Word. In order to partake of these godly promises, we have to first become knowledgeable of these promises, receive them by faith, and then walk according to them.

The Body of Christ is not lacking anything. Everything we need is found in the promises that God made to us. If we are oppressed by corruption, in any form or fashion, we need to look into the promises that are found in the Word and dismiss the oppression. It does not have a right to reign over you. The Bible admonishes us to let not sin reign in our mortal bodies. This indicates that we have the power of choice.

In natural circumstances, the body functions in order when it receives its orders from the head. When the body listens to the head, it becomes all that's in the head. When our bodies decide not to listen to the head, it malfunctions because it was divinely created to function that way. Because it refuses to take its orders from the head, the body may become sick, disoriented, or even lame. In essence, the body is all that's in the head. As goes the natural man, so goes the spiritual man.

Jesus Christ is the Head of the Body of Christ. His desire is for His body to represent or be all that's in the head. Jesus, who is our head, sends messages to His body (the Body of Christ) to inform us of all the exceeding great and precious promises that belong to us so that corruption won't overcome us.

Corruption has no authority over the Word of God; therefore, it has no right to reign over us. In fact, Christ has given the Body of Christ the authority over it. We have a right to dismiss the corruption that is in this world. Just knowing that corruption has no power over us is not enough; we must control it or it will control us.

The law says that we are free from the corruption that is in the world. If we walk in this realm of the Word, when the world sees us, they will see Jesus. Being Christian in this world is that glory and virtue because the Bible clearly states, "As He is, so are we in this world." This is what the world wants to see in us.

When you look into the Word, it's like looking into the mirror. The image in the mirror is yourself. You see yourself, but you don't recognize yourself because what you see is too good to be true. You can see Jesus because you think that He alone can do and be these great things. Jesus told His disciples that the works that I do, shall ye do also and greater works than these shall ye do because I go unto my Father.

When we look into the promises of God, we are supposed to see Jesus and at the same time, we are to keep in mind that Jesus is *our example*! Jesus escaped the corruption in this world. Jesus was not overtaken with anything that the devil had to offer because He knew that He was divinely blessed by God to dominate and to overcome all the corruption in this world. Jesus has given us the same power and authority to tread on serpents and scorpions and over all the power of the enemy and promised that nothing shall by any means hurt us.

God has richly endowed us with everything that we need to escape the moral rot that's in the earth. We are called to glorify God in this earth but we cannot do it living a corrupt life. *So rise up! Body of Christ! Take up thy bed of corruption, and walk in those things that pertain to life and godliness!*

CHAPTER 18

See What the Lord Has Done

2 Corinthians 4: 3&4 states: But if our gospel be hid, it is hid to them that are lost; In whom the god of this world hath blinded the minds of them which believe not, lest the light of the glorious gospel of Christ, who is the image of God, should shine unto them.

According to *Webster's Dictionary*, *blindness* means sightless if you are talking about your ability to see with your eyes, but it also means not using discernment or judgment. One of the most powerful weapons that Satan uses to keep us from receiving what rightfully belongs to us is blindness. If you are blind to a situation, that means that you can't see or discern it. When you're blind, you can't really know where you're going. You will run the risk of running into things unawares. Without a guide, you will possibly get hurt. The world, or the unbeliever, doesn't know that Jesus Christ has already saved and delivered them from Satan's power. Everything that the Body of Christ will ever need is also available to the world, but Satan blinds them to the fact. Jesus died so that the world might be saved. If the world never discerns that fact, they will never receive what the Lord has done for them.

Isaiah 53:5 says that Jesus was wounded for our transgressions, He was bruised for our iniquities, and the chastisement of our peace was upon Him, and by His stripes, we are healed. Salvation is everything that we could ever need to live a happy, successful life. It includes your life, health, wealth, and peace. Most people perceive it as a ticket to heaven, but it is more than that. Salvation means total deliverance from the bondage of Satan (i.e., total deliverance from sin and its consequences).

Everything that brings on destruction or death is the consequence of sin. If destruction comes to you, you don't have to receive it because Christ has already delivered us from it. If you don't see that in His Word, the devil will have a field day.

The biggest problem with the Body of Christ is that we haven't discerned the fact that salvation is a total package; therefore, we have just received parts of it. Somehow we have left our health out. Somehow we left our wealth out, and when we leave those out, we don't have any peace because Satan is using our blindness to the fact that it belongs to us; he is using it against us.

It's time to open up our eyes and *see what the Lord has done*! We have to take the blinders off and see that the Lord has saved us. See that the Lord has healed us. See that the Lord has prospered us! So rise up, Body of Christ! Take the blinders off, and walk in what the Lord has done. If you see that you are healed, then be healed. If you see that you are delivered, then be delivered. If you see that you are prosperous, then be prosperous. Awake, Body of Christ, and see what the Lord has done!

CHAPTER 19

Don't Believe the Lie

The Bible tells us, "Ye shall know the truth and the truth shall make you free." If you want to know the truth about a situation, go to the Word of God. If you give God's Word preeminence over all, there is no way that you will get caught up in Satan's lies. If you don't believe the lies that Satan tells you, then he has no power over you. Satan is defenseless to the truth. Satan already knows that the only way to defeat a lie, which is what he is, is with the truth. A *lie* is defined in *Webster's Dictionary* as an assertion of something known or believed by the speaker to be untrue with the intent to deceive; something that misleads or deceives; to create a false impression. One of Satan's greatest weapons is deception.

If you know that the devil is a lie, then why do we believe him? A lie is anything against God's Word. The Body of Christ needs to stop buying the devil's wolf tickets. He uses wolf tickets to frighten us into believing and acting on his lies. If we had not believed the lie in the beginning, we wouldn't have had to experience it. That's why God told us to cast down every imagination and every high thing that exalts itself against the knowledge of God, bringing into captivity every thought to the obedience of Christ.

John 8:44 states, "Ye are of your father the devil, and the lusts of your father ye will do. He was a murderer from the beginning, and abode not in the truth, because there is no truth in him. When he speaketh a lie, he speaketh of his own; for he is a liar, and the father of it."

I asked the question, where did sickness and disease come from, or what is the origin of it? The one thing I do know is that it didn't come from God. The answer is that it originated from the lies that Satan coerced Eve and Adam to believe. It came as a result of their disobedience, which caused the curse in the Garden of Eden, which came upon the whole earth and mankind.

Adam and Eve were in perfect health before the fall. God never intended for us to be sick. Jesus, our King, told us in Jeremiah 29:11, "For I know the thoughts that I think toward you, saith the Lord, thoughts of peace, *and not of evil*, to give you an expected end."

Sickness and disease are killers of the powers of darkness. It came to steal, kill, and destroy us, but our Lord and Savior, Jesus Christ, came that we might have life and have it more abundantly.

Sickness and disease are designed to hinder the plan of God in our lives. Knowing the origin of it helps us to know how to deal with it. This liar, Satan, tells us that we have to die with something. Don't believe that lie. Cast it down. Jesus stated in 1 Peter 2:24, "Who His own self bare our sins in his own body on the tree, that we, being dead to sins, should live unto righteousness, by whose stripes ye were healed."

We need to confess divine health every day because Jesus bought and paid for us to have it. It may be a fact that you have been stricken with a disease, but the truth says that by the stripes of Jesus, we are healed. We have to decide whose report we are going to believe. Having faith in what Jesus bought and paid for us to have will eradicate sickness and disease. So we must agree with God and not Satan.

Psalm 107:20 states, "He sent His Word, and healed them, and delivered them from their destructions." We have to believe the Word of God and don't take it down. We need to declare, "No weapon formed against me shall prosper and every tongue that rises up against me, I will condemn it."

We are not at Satan's mercy anymore. We have been delivered from his power. Colossians 1:13 states, "Who [Christ] hath delivered us from the power of darkness, and hath translated us into the kingdom of His [God's] dear Son [Jesus]." We have the right to deny Satan's right to put sickness and disease on us. We are no longer under the rule of Satan, nor are we citizens of his kingdom. When we were born again, we became citizens of the kingdom of God, thereby, under new rulership of a new King, and that's Jesus Himself. We have to come to the knowledge that the rules of the old kingdom of Satan no longer apply to us. We, the children of the kingdom of God, are governed by the rules and laws of the kingdom of God.

We should treat sickness and disease like an armed robber because it comes to steal, kill, and destroy. Attack it with your faith in the Word of God because His Word is life to those who find it and health to all their flesh.

Don't believe everything you see because sometimes it's not what it looks like. If you fill your whole house with God, then there is no place for anything else. If I believed in everything I see with my natural eyes, then I would have no need of faith. Faith is the substance of things hoped for and the evidence of things not seen. You can't see faith, but you can see a manifestation of faith. Everything you see in the natural is a manifestation of somebody's faith in action, whether it is good or bad. Your lives exemplify what you have faith in. If your life consists of things that you really don't want, then you need to redirect your faith. We have had a hard time getting to the place of being filled with God because we are spending too much time giving place to what our eyes see. You are just beating at the wind.

Regroup! Rethink this thing. Stop buying the devil's wolf tickets. What is a wolf-ticket? It is a common-sense lie. It's something that seems logical to believe. For example, "I am just an old sinner saved by grace, you have to die with something, once an alcoholic always an alcoholic, once a drug addict, always a drug addict." If you believe this, then you will never receive your deliverance from them. All of these conditions came about as a result of the curse. My brothers and sisters, Christ has delivered us from these things. *Lies, lies, lies! Don't believe the lies! Rise up from these beds of lies from the devil and walk in the truth of God's Word!*

CHAPTER 20

It Is Finished

Jesus knew that we didn't know the Father as we should have during His earthly ministry. He did everything possible to reveal the Father to us. He didn't come to reveal Himself. In revealing the Father to us, He healed the sick, raised the dead, cast out demons, preached the Gospel to the poor, fed five thousand, spoke to the storm, turned water into wine, delivered us, loved us, and saved us.

In every demonstration that Jesus did, He dominated the law of sin and death. Nothing could overcome Him nor overtake Him. He thoroughly demonstrated the power of God. Jesus didn't put a lot of work into anything that He did. He just spoke the Word of God to every circumstance, and the manifestation of the word that He spoke showed up. These were the true works of God, and He expects that when we come into the knowledge of the truth, we should walk therein.

Jesus did His part, and now *it's on us.* When Jesus hung on the cross, He cried out, "It is finished!" He was letting the world know that He had done what He had come to do. *Mission accomplished!* He fulfilled His destiny. Now the question is, what are we going to do? I can tell you what God wants us to do, and that is to rise up and do what He did. He was saying, "I have made a way for you, I have set you free, and I have paid the price for your sin."

Jesus said to His disciples, "The works that I do shall ye do also, and greater works than these shall you do because I go to My Father."

Now it is time for us to go and represent the Father just like Jesus did. So what are we going to do? *We are going to do what Jesus did! So rise up, take up thy bed, and walk!*

CHAPTER 21

Living the Life

The purpose of Jesus's coming was so we could live an abundant life. Jesus says, "I am come that ye might have life, and that you might have it more abundantly." The understanding of the Scripture will take us to a higher level of being, which will take us to a higher level of living. In fact, it will take us to a level that's well above just being alive. Being alive could mean just existing. But Jesus didn't come that we might live, but that we might have Life, Zoe Life, and plenty of it.

Just being alive is existing with a death sentence attached to it. It can be expressed in words as the living dead. That was the state of man after the fall in the Garden of Eden. God warned man that the day he ate from the Tree of the Knowledge of Good and Evil, he would surely die.

But thank God! Jesus said that I came that we might have Life (Zoe Life) and that we might have it more abundantly. Jesus said, "I set before you life and death, blessing and cursing. You choose." *Jesus gave us our life back, so choose life, people of God! So rise up and live!*

WISDOM FOR THE SISTERS

Sisters, you are God's prized creations. He took the time and built you for Adam. He made you to be a blessing to him and not a curse. God has given us the power of influence. Don't allow the devil to use you against the Adams in this world. God made you to help him up and not cause him to fall. We know that a good man loves his woman. The glory of the man is his woman. He will pay big money for her and will even sacrifice his life for her if he wants her bad enough. Satan has used us to cause millions of men to lose their lives and their positions with God. I am not saying that we are his problem, but that from the beginning of time, the devil used Eve to get Adam, and that brought sin into this world, and Satan is yet using that same tactic to destroy us, especially the church.

The power of influence from a beautiful woman who is yielded to Satan is a powerful weapon against a man. Don't let that woman be you. Ladies, we know that we have what the brothers need, so be a wise woman and give it to the right brother, and that's your husband. Stop casting your pearls before swine and give no place to the devil.

Ladies, if we would rise up and dress presentably in modest apparel and not like hoochies on the streets and rid ourselves of promiscuity and teach our daughters the art of chastity, we will become a tremendous blessing to our men and our God. They will treat us like queens when we act like queens. When we begin to see ourselves as queens and realize our value, then the devil will be defenseless against us. We will not be a pawn in his hand to use any longer.

The devil used our power of influence against Adam. When that happened, the whole creation fell. God created us to bless and not to curse.

The same doorway that man has to come through in this world is the same doorway the devil uses to take man out of this world. When you turn on the television, what do you see? A woman portrayed as a sex object. Sisters, we have to show the world that we are not sex objects but that we are God's woman, the Bride of Christ, a Proverbs 31 woman.

Women, don't let the devil use you any longer. If you want to know how the mighty have fallen, ask Adam, ask the president. Every time a man rises to power, the devil already knows the perfect tool to use to bring him down. He'll always find him a woman.

God calls us the helpmeet, which means he created us to help meet his needs. When we rise up and let the devil know that he's not going to use us any longer, we will become a blessing to our man and will help him progress so that he will reign as kings and we will reign as queens. When the man rises up, his woman rises with him.

Ladies, can't you see that the devil knows the power that we have? Instead of allowing ourselves to go against man, let's go against Satan. The Bible says that the seed of the woman would bruise Satan's head. The head is equivalent to Satan's authority. Women, let's declare war on Satan and pull him down. We have suffered long enough for our mistake. Now it's time to put Satan in his place, and that's under our feet.

Sisters, the major attack is not really against you but it is against the man because God has made him the head of his family and the church. Satan knows that women can be irresistible, so he will use you to get to the man's head. Satan knows that if he can get to your head (the man), he already got you.

God is looking for the example of Esther and Ruth in this world (i.e., women who know how to submit herself to her king, a woman who knows how to carry herself before all kings, a woman who is a good example before all queens), but most of all, He is looking for a woman who knows how and strives to please the King of kings.

Sisters, let's rise up and use the devil's head as a platform and loose ourselves from his influence and walk.

WISDOM FOR THE BROTHERS

Brothers, you are made in God's image. That is why the devil will try to destroy you. God has made you the head of His estate. In Psalm 8:4–6, a question was asked: "What is man, that thou art mindful of him? And the son of man, that thou visitest him? For thou hast made him a little lower than the angels, and hast crowned him with glory and honour. Thou madest him to have dominion over the works of thy hands; thou hast put all things under his feet." You have been placed in a very high position, a place of authority, with the job description according to Genesis 1:27–28, which states, "So God created man in his own image, in the image of God created he him; male and female created he them. And God blessed them, and God said unto them, Be fruitful, and multiply, and replenish the earth, and subdue it: and have dominion over the fish of the sea, and over the fowl of the air, and over every living thing that moveth upon the earth." The devil desires to have that position. Satan is mad at God for kicking him out of heaven, and to get back at God, he tries to mess up His prized possession, and that's you. Adam lost his position with God, but Jesus gave it back, and the devil has been trying very hard to take it again.

Brothers, don't be ignorant of Satan's devices. His tactics have not changed. He is still using women against you. He is after your headship, which is your place of authority. Brothers, you have what it takes to overcome that devil. Take advice from Ephesians 6:10–18, which states, "Finally, my brethren, be strong in the Lord and in the power of His might." He also told Joshua to "be strong and very courageous." He also told you in 1 Peter 5:8 to "be sober, be vigilant; because your adversary the devil, as a roaring lion, walketh about, seeking whom he may devour."

God is looking for men who know how to flee the very appearance of evil. Like Joseph, don't fall prey to Potiphar's wife or the Jezebels that are coming your way. Resist and flee, even if it strips you. And if she lies on you, don't worry because a lie will die, and God will stand up for you.

Be strong, my brothers, and rise up, take up thy bed, and walk!

My Prayer for You

Colossians 1:9–11 states, "For this cause we also, since the day we heard it, do not cease to pray for you, and to desire that you might be filled with the knowledge of his will in all wisdom and spiritual understanding; That you might *walk* worthy of the Lord unto all pleasing, being fruitful in every good work, and increasing in the knowledge of God; Strengthened with all might, according to his glorious power, unto all patience and longsuffering with joyfulness."

The apostle Paul had a personal encounter with the Lord. He was a very zealous, well-educated man who killed for what he believed because he thought that he was taught by the best. But when he came into contact with Jesus Christ, it was a life-changing experience! He stated that he would give it all up just to know this Man called Jesus the Christ.

Philippians 3:7–10 states that the apostle Paul said, "But what things were gain to me, those I counted loss for Christ: Yea, doubtless, and I count all things but loss for the excellency of the knowledge of Christ Jesus my Lord; for whom I have suffered the loss of all things, and do count them but dung; that I may win Christ; and be found in him, not having mine own righteousness, which is of the law, but that which is through the faith of Christ, the righteousness which is of God by faith; That I may know him, and the power of his resurrection, and the fellowship of his sufferings, being made conformable unto his death."

Paul experienced the excellency of the knowledge of the Glory of God in such a way that he prayed that we would have the same experience. He was telling us that "you have got to know Him and the power of His resurrection. This is the desire of the Father's heart for all of his sons and daughters." Jesus wanted this life for us so badly that he paid the price with his life. Jesus gave it all! And the Apostle Paul got to know Jesus and found that knowing Him was more glorious and the life that he knew was no comparison.

Romans 8:18 says, "For I reckon that the sufferings of this present time are not worthy to be compared with the glory which shall be revealed in us; so yes, we are going to suffer some, but it's going to be worth it. The reward is going to be so much greater."

So rise up, my sisters and brothers in Christ, put away all fear, and walk!

Prayer of Salvation and Baptism in the Holy Spirit

Heavenly Father, I come to You in the name of Jesus! I have read in Your Word in Acts 2:21 that whoever calls on the name of the Lord shall be saved. According to Romans 10:9–10, "If you shall confess with your mouth the Lord Jesus, and shall believe in your heart that God has raised Him from the dead, you shall be saved. For with the heart one believes unto righteousness; and with the mouth, confession is made unto salvation."

Lord, I believe that Jesus died for my sins, and I believe that He was raised from the dead. I repent of my sins. Come into my heart, Lord Jesus, and be Lord of my life.

I am now a born-again child of God. I am a new creature in Christ Jesus, and I renounce the devil and everything he stands for. Lord, thank you for saving me. In Luke 11:13, You said, "If you then, being evil, know how to give good gifts unto your children, how much more shall your heavenly Father give the Holy Spirit to those who ask Him?" I am asking for this most needed gift: fill me, Lord! I receive Him into my life now, in Jesus's name.

What Now?

Romans 12:1–2 says, "I beseech you therefore, brethren, by the mercies of God, that ye present your bodies a living sacrifice, holy, acceptable unto God, which is your reasonable service. And be not conformed to this world; but be ye transformed by the renewing of your mind, that ye may prove what is that good, and acceptable, and perfect will of God."

Find a Word-teaching church. Be fed the milk of the word so you can grow. Read the Bible for yourself. *Pray, pray, pray.* Stay in communion with God so you can rise up and walk in this new life that Jesus has provided for us!

NOTE

About the Author

Dr. Denice Jacklin Valentine was born to the late Henrietta D. Blackstock and the late Thomas Allen of Eden, North Carolina. Denice is a mother of two—Lt. Col. Marvin Blackstock and Minister Chad Blackstock. She is married to Earnest L. Valentine Sr. and is a stepmother of three—Cotina, Nyree, and Leroy Jr.

Dr. Denice was educated at the Jacksonville Theological Seminary where she received a PhD in clinical Christian counseling.

Dr. Denice is a cofounder (along with her husband) of Ambassadors for Christ Ministries of Eden, North Carolina. She is a well-respected woman of God, an educator with a compassion to share the gospel of Jesus Christ to set the captives free by the Word of God. Dr. Denice, a messenger with a message from the King of kings and with an assignment to get the Church up, has spoken at many conferences with a driving purpose to teach others to rise up and walk in the blessings that Jesus has already provided for us at Calvary.

www.ingramcontent.com/pod-product-compliance
Lightning Source LLC
LaVergne TN
LVHW091442070125
800705LV00002B/215